PASS!

NO PUPPY GUARDING!

Written by Lindsay & Seth Little

Illustrated by Daniel Gill

Meyer & Meyer Sport

British Library Cataloguing in Publication Data

A catalogue record for this book is available from the British Library

Pass! No Puppy Guarding!

Aachen, Auckland, Beirut, Cairo, Cape Town, Dubai, Hägendorf, Hong Kong, Indianapolis, Manila, New Delhi, Singapore, Sydney, Tehran, Vienna

Member of the World Sport Publishers' Association (WSPA)

Manufacturing: Print Consult GmbH, Munich, Germany

ISBN 978-1-78255-100-3
E-Mail: info@m-m-sports.com, service@learnsportbooks.com
www.m-m-sports.com
www.learnsportbooks.com

May 2016

My Life in Soccer

by Yael Averbuch

Soft, green grass. Fun times with my family. Love and joy. Those are some of the first things that come to mind when I think about soccer.

I was seven years old when I watched my first soccer game. I didn't know anything about the sport besides that it seemed fun. My best friend in school invited me to come watch her game and my dad took me to cheer for her. That day, her team needed extra players and they asked me if I would play. I was very shy and said no. After watching her game, though, I decided that it looked like a lot of fun so my dad signed me up to play on a recreational team the next season.

I fell in love with the game at my first soccer practice, and have loved it ever since. It was a special time to share with my dad, as we learned about the game together. It was fun to be out on the field with my teammates and getting to play. And it was a whole new set of skills and experiences that made me very excited to learn.

When I was nine I wrote in my journal that I wanted to be a professional soccer player. I didn't really understand at the time what that meant, and

I certainly didn't know what it would take to get there. But I knew that I wanted to play for as long as I could and be the best I could be.

Since that time, soccer has taken me all across the world. I have played all over the U.S., in England, Germany, Holland, Japan, China, Australia, New Zealand, Thailand, Mexico, Canada, Sweden, Russia, Serbia and many other countries! I have also played for my country. I have formed friendships playing soccer that will last a lifetime. I have also learned a lot about myself through the game. I have learned what it takes to be a champion, and also how to overcome disappointments along the way.

Soccer is called "the beautiful game." There are so many reasons the sport is so beautiful and I'm sure that you will understand them as you play. I love soccer because there is such a variety of skills to learn. There are physical skills (like running fast, being strong, playing aggressively), skills with the ball (dribbling, trapping, shooting), and skills like teamwork and leadership. All are important to the game. There is no one right way to play soccer. It is a game of imagination and creativity.

I am now living the dream I have had since I was nine years old. I am a professional soccer player. It has not always been an easy path to accomplish my goals, but whenever I practice or play, I continue to love soccer more than ever.

Soon after I started playing, my dad and I began a mission to learn the game together. We would watch videos of soccer training and try to do the same drills in my backyard. I hope that you will enjoy learning and practicing the same way I did then, and have continued to do all my career.

I encourage you to learn and play the game of soccer, but most importantly, have fun while you do!

Learn more about Yael Averbuch on her website: www.yaelaverbuch.com
Yael is also the founder of the Techne Futbol Training System, which helps players develop the skills necessary to play soccer and have fun: www.technefutbol.com

My name is Bailee Kate, but everyone just calls me B.

I love to play soccer! This is my second year playing soccer on a real team. This season we even have matching uniforms and our own numbers!

We are The Mighty Minions!

This is my dog, Thor. He is so cute!

Sometimes he comes to soccer practice. He likes to chase the ball around just like my team!

In our soccer games my team tries to score goals by kicking the ball into the other team's goal. When we try to score the other team plays **defense**! They try to get in our way and stop us from scoring. They try to take the ball away from us.

We play **defense** when the other team has the ball. Coach says that the best way to play **defense** is to get in the path of the other team.

He said we should stay between the ball and our goal. Coach calls this being **goal-side**.

I think that is a really funny-sounding word!

Sometimes I think Thor plays defense for the other team because he is always in my way! He gets in trouble at practice because he gets in my way when I am trying to dribble or pass the ball to my teammates.

Coach says that sometimes I act just like Thor because I get in my own teammates' way. When one of my teammates has the ball and I get in his way, Coach calls it **puppy guarding**.

Coach teaches us that **puppy guarding** does not help our team. I think he should tell that to Thor too!

Coach knows my team likes to chase the ball, but he tells us to spread out when our team has the ball. He says that we will score more goals if we spread out on the field and pass the ball to each other.

Coach tells us to **open up** when he wants us to move away from each other and spread out on the field.

When my team **opens up** we have more room to dribble the ball, pass to a teammate and even score a goal!

Coach tells me that when I spread out and no one from the other team is near me, I need to yell *pass* or *ball*! That way my teammate with the ball knows that I am open.

When I have the ball I try to look up to see where my teammates are on the field so I can pass to them if they are open. When I pass the ball to my teammate, she should control it and make sure the other team cannot steal it from her.

11

Today we have a big soccer game! We are playing against the Yellow Dragons. They are fierce!

Last season they didn't just beat us—they beat us up! The Yellow Dragons are an aggressive team. They all run toward the ball as fast as they can and take it away from whoever has it!

Right before we run onto the field, Coach circles us together and reminds us not to **puppy guard** each other. He tells us to play **defense** when we don't have the ball and reminds us to get our body **goal-side** between the Yellow Dragons and our goal.

Then we put our hands in for our big team yell. It is fun to yell so loud! I love it!

Once the game starts we play tough, but the Yellow Dragons keep ganging up on us.

Whenever we have the ball, they swarm around the ball like bees. They kick at the ball until they get it back.

We play **goal-side defense** and steal the ball from them too. It looks like nobody will be able to score a goal in this game!

Suddenly, the Yellow Dragons plow through all of us and are about to score a goal. At the last second my teammate, Brody, gets his body **goal-side** to slow them down. Then my other teammate, Jett, steals the ball from the Yellow Dragons.

The Yellow Dragons circle around Jett. I start **puppy guarding** him too because I want the ball. Then I hear coach yell, “Open up please. No **puppy guarding**!”

I run away from Jett to create some space. None of the Yellow Dragons follow me! They don't care where I am going since I don't have the ball!

At first Jett can't see me because the Yellow Dragons are surrounding him.

No Yellow Dragons are near me, so I yell, "*Ball*, *ball*, *pass*!" as loud as I can. Jett hears me. He looks up and passes the ball right to me!

All of the Yellow Dragons run to surround me. I hear my teammate Elijah yell "*Pass*, B!" I look up and pass the ball to him as fast as I can. None of the Yellow Dragons are as fast as the ball when we pass to each other.

Elijah dribbles the ball straight toward
their goal and scores with a rocket kick!

Everybody cheers!
My team celebrates!

When I get home after the game,
I hug Thor with a big squeeze.

I am so happy we scored against
the Yellow Dragons!

Teaching Concepts & Vocabulary

Puppy guarding: A player is "puppy guarding" when he gets in his teammate's way while his team controls the ball. This crowding prevents teammates from playing the ball by dribbling or passing it into a more attacking position.

Open up: Players open up when teammates move away from one another on the field and look to receive a pass. This creates more space to pass and receive the ball in more attacking positions.

Goal-side: On defense, players position themselves goal-side by moving between their own goal and the other team's attacking players so they can prevent goals by blocking a shot or stealing the ball.

EAT THE RIGHT THINGS!

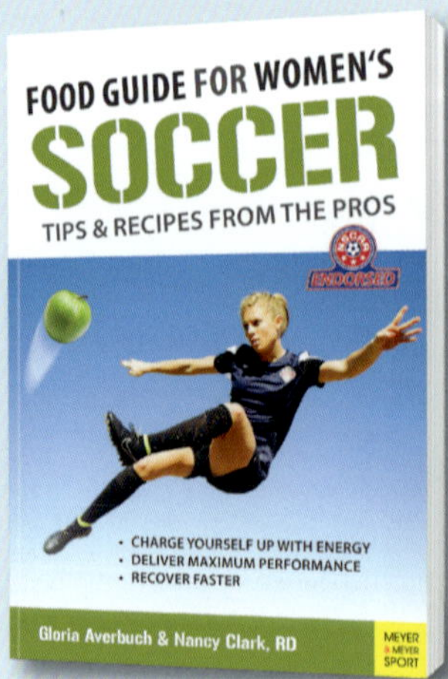

Averbuch/Clark, RD

FOOD GUIDE FOR WOMEN'S SOCCER

TIPS & RECIPES FROM THE PROS

Soccer players are hungry for good nutrition information. This easy-to-read book offers practical tips, debunks nutrition myths, and is a simple "how-to" resource for soccer players, their coaches and parents. Professional soccer players offer advice along with recipes and sample menus.

256 p., in color,
40 photos, 41 illus.,
paperback, 6 ½" x 9 ¼"

ISBN: 9781782550518

$ 18.95 US/$ 32.95 AUS
£ 14.95 UK/€18.95